On Christmas day your red star is complete. Add five gold pipe cleaners to make it sparkle.

2 Shoes for Santa

The story of Santa Claus is the story of Saint Nicholas. He wanted to help a poor family so he threw gold coins down their chimney. The gold fell in the stockings and shoes left by the fire.

Saint Nicholas' Day is December 6. One tradition is to put out shoes the night before. By the morning, they are filled with sweets and gifts!

Another tradition is to hang stockings out on Christmas Eve.

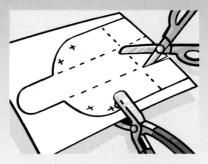

1 Cut the shoe shape out of thin card. Punch holes for the laces.

2 Paint the card. When it is dry, add fingerprint dots or draw a pattern with a marker pen.

3 Fold up the flaps as shown. Glue in place.

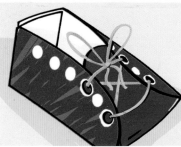

4 Add the laces and tie them in a bow.

I can make things for Christmas

Words and crafts by
Christina Goodings

Photography by John Williams
Illustration by Adrian Barclay

Contents

LION
CHILDREN'S

1 Advent calendar

Advent is the time to get ready for Christmas. This calendar helps you count the days in December until Christmas Day on December 25.

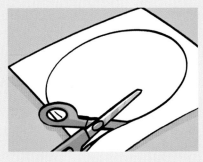

1 Cut a circle in thin white card.

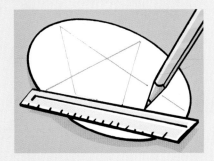

2 Draw a five pointed star with the points not quite at the edge. Use a yellow pencil crayon and a ruler.

3 Paint the star yellow.

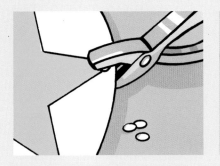

4 Punch a hole at each of the star's points.

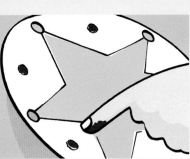

5 Put a dab of red paint in a saucer. Dip one fingertip in. Make a red fingerprint in each of the five white spaces.

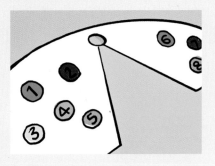

6 Do the same with orange, yellow, green and blue paint. On the first of December write '1' on a fingerprint. Add a number each day.

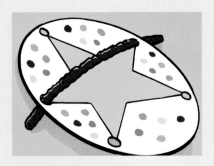

7 After 5 days put in one red pipecleaner along a straight edge of the star, from hole to hole.

8 Do the same with the next spaces to count all 25 days.

5 fingerprints in each of 5 spaces makes 25 fingerprints — one for every day of the calendar.

This full size template is easy to copy.

Do not paint this area – it will glue better if left plain.

Do not paint this area – it will glue better if left plain.

3 Nativity scene

'Nativity' means birth. Christmas is a religious festival, celebrating the birth of Jesus. The people who follow Jesus call him 'Christ', which means 'chosen king'. They believe he is God's son.

A nativity scene shows baby Jesus in a manger, his mother Mary and Joseph.

Shepherds come to find the newborn king.

Wise men follow a star and come with gifts.

1 Cut a rectangle of card 42cm x 15cm. Use a ruler to help you mark the top and bottom points of six equal sections.

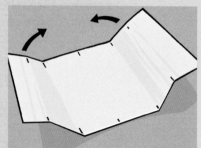

2 Use the marks to fold the card. Fold the left side in as shown and then the right side.

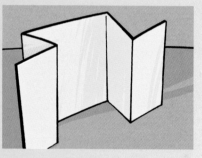

3 Fold again to make the doors. If you like, cut the fully folded card into a roof shape.

4 On plain white paper, draw outlines for the people in the nativity scene. Colour them in.

5 Cut out your people. Glue them in place.

6 Add a star above and whatever other decorations you would like!

Baby Jesus lies in a manger of straw.

Joseph and the shepherds wear tunics and cloaks.

Mary the mother wears blue.

Wise men wear expensive robes.

4 Christmas angels

Angels play their part in the story of the nativity.
   An angel tells Mary she is going to have a baby.
   Angels tell shepherds that a baby has been born in Bethlehem.
   In the Christian tradition, an angel is a messenger from
God in heaven. People imagine them flying to earth.

1 Take a rectangle of paper about 80cm x 50cm and fold it in half.

2 Draw a wing shape. Cut it out through both layers and unfold the paper.

3 Lay the wing shape on thin card and draw round it. Cut out card wings.

4 Paint a design in gold on the wings. Add extra decorations with gold or glitter pens.

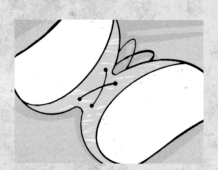

5 Punch two sets of two holes. Thread a length of gold elastic through each pair. Tie each in a loop so you can wear the wings like a backpack.

These wings are decorated with acrylic paint: the centre part was brushed and the rest was sponged (see page 6).

5 Christmas star

In the story of the nativity, wise men follow a star in the hope of finding a king. It leads them to Bethlehem, and to Jesus.

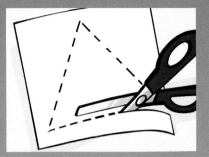

1 Draw a triangle with sides exactly the same length on thin card. Cut it out.

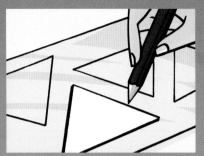

2 Draw round the shape on strong paper to make as many stars as you want. Cut out the triangles.

3 Paint your triangles on both sides. You can use the same colour or different colours on each side.

4 Fold the top point to the bottom edge.

5 In the same way, fold the left point to the right edge. Then fold the right point to the left edge.

Decorate your stars with gold
and silver marker pens or glue
on glitter or sequins.
Use thread to hang them on
the tree or from the ceiling.

Make the stars out of
coloured paper if you don't
want to spend time painting
them.

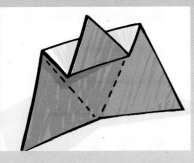

6 Unfold the star. Then
refold each point and
half fold backwards.

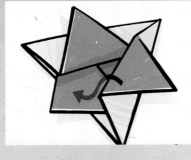

7 Interweave the folds.

6 Evergreens

Evergreen trees keep their leaves though the season when other trees look dead. They are a Christian symbol of God's undying love.

Evergreens with bright berries are Christmassy. Another way to add colour is to tie ribbons or pipe cleaners to the twigs.

1 Brush gesso all over a terracotta pot. Leave it to dry.

2 Dip a sponge into gold acrylic paint. Press it once onto a piece of kitchen towel to blot it.

3 Press the sponge onto the pot to make a mottled pattern. Dip, blot and press as many times as you need to cover the pot.

4 Brush a band of gold around the rim.

5 When the paint is dry, cut a circle of card to fit in the bottom of the pot. Fill it with damp sand.

6 Arrange evergreen twigs in the pot.

7 Christmas gifts

The wise men brought Jesus gifts: gold, frankincense and myrrh. Giving gifts at Christmas is a way of remembering the story of the nativity. It is also a way of telling someone that you love them.

1 Select a cardboard box and paint it all over with gesso.

2 Cut a strip of paper to wrap round the box once like a ribbon band plus about 10cm extra.

3 Mix your chosen colour of paint with white (PVA) glue and paint your box and your band. Let them dry so you can add decorations.

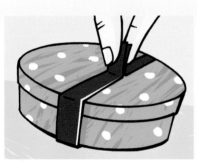

4 To fit the band, wrap it round the box so the ends meet. Hold the ends with one finger and thumb and use your other finger and thumb to hold the band tight to the box. Crease.

Swirl a mixture of colours over the box using your hands like a giant paintbrush.

5 Now take the band off the box and lay it flat. Make a cut halfway UP one crease and halfway DOWN the other.

6 Put the band on the box, and slot the two slits together to join them.

Use a paintbrush to add a decoration all round the edge.

Use your fingers to add coloured fingerprint dots.

8 Snowball treats

Make these sweet treats to share.

They make a great gift: the wrapping idea on page 9 works perfectly.

Remember to ask a grown up before you do any cooking. Then wash your hands and turn the oven to 150C.

1 Put 150g caster sugar in a bowl with 150g ground almonds. Mix.

2 Grate the rind from 1 orange. Add this to the mixture.

3 Add 1 teaspoon of vanilla essence and 1 egg white. Mix.

4 Squeeze in just enough orange juice to make a sticky dough.

Squeeze some orange juice onto a saucer and dip the cherries or almonds in to help them stick.

5 Put icing sugar on a plate. Drop spoonfuls of dough into the sugar and roll them around.

6 Line a baking tray with parchment. Arrange the snowballs on the tray.

7 Decorate with glace cherries or almonds. Bake for 10 minutes.

9 Gift wrap

1 Take a sheet of plain white paper. Crumple it and uncrumple it several times. Then press it smooth.

2 Mix paint with a little white (PVA) glue and water. Brush it over the paper. When it dries, brush on a second coat and let that dry too.

3 Put another colour paint on a flat plate in a thin layer.

A cardboard tube makes prints just like a cookie cutter. Can you think of other things to print with?

4 Dip a cookie cutter in the paint and then press it onto the paper. Do this over and over again to make a pattern. Leave to dry.

5 Place your gift on the paper like this. Fold up the bottom edge.

6 Fold over one side and then the other.

7 Tie the top with a pipe cleaner or ribbon.

10 Gifts on the tree

Hang tiny treats on the Christmas tree so everyone can have a gift!

Have a party and ask everyone to put a real coin in a gift bag when they have taken their treat. After Christmas, you can give the money to a good cause.

1 Cut a square of paper, about 20cm x 20cm. Paint one side in a bright colour. Leave to dry.

2 Paint the other side with a metallic paint and leave to dry.

3 Place the paper metallic side up. Fold the lower point to the upper point and crease.

4 Bend the right edge to the bottom fold. Crease and unfold.

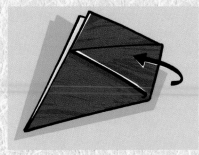

5 Take the right point and fold it to where the crease meets the left edge.

6 Fold the left side to match.

7 Fold upper layer of the top point forwards and the lower layer backwards.

Pull a length of thread under the crease and tie it in a loop to hang the bag.

11 Christmas greetings

Send a Christmas message to someone near or far. Tell them how much you love them.

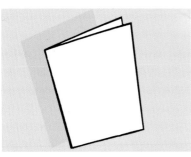

1 Choose a rectangle of thin card. Fold it in half and crease the fold.

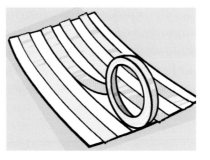

2 Put strips of masking tape down the card.

3 Use a stiff brush to dab paint along the strips of card left showing. Let it almost dry.

4 Gently pull the masking tape away. Decorate the plain strips left with marker pens.

Each time you pull a strip of masking tape, press it against a piece of cotton cloth to take away some of the stickiness.

5 Decorate two pieces of paper in different colours to match the card you have made. Fold each one in half.

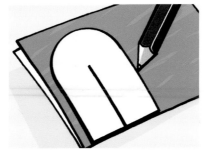

6 Cut the template below in thin card. Draw round the shape as shown on each of the folded pieces. Cut them out.

7 Cut the slit up the middle. Interweave your heart pieces to make a little bag. Glue the heart inside the card.

You can write a message to put inside the heart.

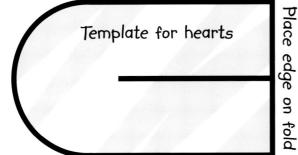

Template for hearts

Place edge on fold

12 Tree cards

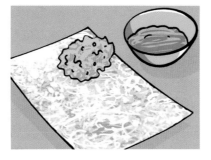

1 Choose a rectangle of thin card. Fold it in half and crease the fold. Unfold.

2 Put some light blue paint in a dish. Dip in a sponge and dab it once on kitchen towel. Dab over the card.

3 Decorate paper for the trees. Smear green all over the paper as a base.

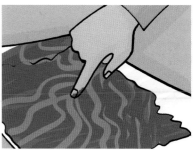

4 Use your fingers to make other patterns as you mix in yellow, blue or white.

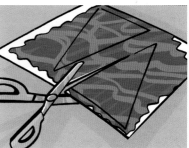

5 Cut tall triangles from your patterned paper. Glue onto the card.

13 Christmas party

Making paper chains is best done with lots of people to help and do the bit they're good at. It's a party just making them!

Begin by cutting the shape given here in card (if you have a lot of people have more than one shape to draw round).

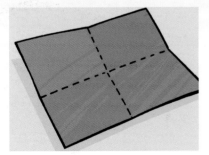

1 For each link, take a piece of paper about 20cm x 10cm. Fold it in half from bottom to top. Fold again from left to right.

2 Draw round the shape on the folded paper, taking care to match the correct edge to the folds.

3 Cut out the paper link. Make lots.

4 Thread the links
together.

Template for chains

The coloured edges line up
with folds in the paper.

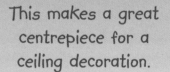

This makes a great centrepiece for a ceiling decoration.

14 Golden lantern

1 Choose metallic card. Paint the plain side gold or a colour.

2 Cut strips about 3cm x 20cm.

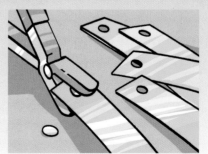

3 Punch holes at each end.

Use curling gift ribbon to decorate your lantern and to hang it.

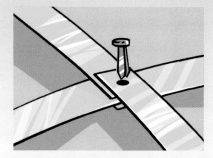

4 Thread one end of each of four strips onto a metal paper fastener, painted side upwards. Use glue or double-sided tape between each layer to keep them square.

5 Fold the strips up so the metallic side faces outwards. Thread the holes on another metal paper fastener.

6 Make a heart from paper foil (see page 11 for how to make hearts). Punch a hole and thread gift ribbon. Tie it inside the lantern.

15 Tabletop trees

Decorate the Christmas table with tiny trees.
You could make one for each place at the table and hide
a tiny wrapped gift under each tree.

Add a star. Cut two
matching shapes in foil
and glue them to a
cocktail stick.

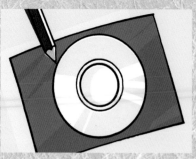

1 Draw round a dinner plate on green paper. Cut out the circle.

2 Fold the circle in half and cut along the fold. Fold one half circle into a cone. Glue and staple in place.

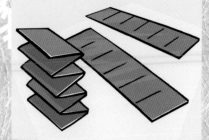

3 Take strips of green paper about 4cm wide. Fold them in zigzags of 1cm each.

4 Cut the folded paper as shown. Snip to make 'leaves'. If you can't cut through all folds at once, just take 2 or 3 at a time.

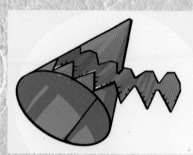

5 Unfold the strips. Glue one round the lower part of the tree, with the leaf tips just touching the bottom edge.

6 Glue another strip above the first, half overlapping the first row. Add more rows in the same way.

7 Cut a small circle in metallic foil. Snip to the centre and fold in place round the top of the tree.

8 Brush glue on the 'leaves', and sprinkle with glitter.

16 Christingle

The Christingle is a symbol of some of the most important things Christians believe.

The orange is the world God made.

The fruits and sweets are the good things God gives.

The red ribbon is a symbol of God's encircling love.

The candle is a symbol of Jesus, who once said 'I am the light of the world'.

A lit Christingle is a lovely table decoration for Christmas day.

Ask a grown-up to be in charge of lighting the candle.

1 Cut the base off an orange so it will stand steady on a small saucer.

2 Use an apple corer to cut a small hole in the top for the candle.

3 Take a red ribbon or strip of paper and glue it round the orange.

4 Skewer dried fruits or sweets on 4 cocktail sticks and stick them in the orange.

5 Add a candle.